AZTEC MYTHOLOGY

*Gods, Heroes, Legends and Myths of the
Aztec Peoples*

By Jim Barrow

To thank you for your purchase, we're offering a free PDF exclusively for the readers of Aztec Mythology: Gods, Heroes, Legends and Myths of the Aztec Peoples.

Dive into the Ancient Civilization and their Gods: Reveal the Secrets of the Egyptian Civilization Going Back 5000 Years B.C. & Learn the Myths That Created their Culture.

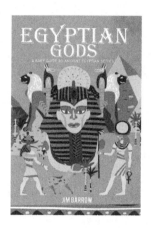

Scan the following QR Code to access your free gift!

CONTENTS

Introduction of the Aztecs

The Aztecs were a group of people that once lived and ruled in southern Mexico. They were around during the 15th and early 16th century, and were well-known for their agriculture, intelligence and productivity, which in turn made them a very prosperous empire rivalled by nobody else during their time until they were conquered by the Spanish.

Interestingly enough, nobody knows quite where the Aztecs came from, but there are various theories that we will dive into over the course of this book. Unfortunately, they eventually fell victim to war and disease, their culture and ways almost disappearing from the world completely.

The Spaniards took over the Aztec kingdom, and they tried to completely destroy the footprint that they left on the world. However, over time historians and archaeologists have been able to piece together their society as their conquerors were not able to quite destroy everything.

What is left of their civilisation can still be seen in some places today and it is truly fascinating how such a large city was able to thrive. Over the course of this book, we are going to review this lost civilisation and explore how incredible the Aztecs were, and how their prosperous empire crumbled.

Chapter One
Background and Overview

History

The Aztec history is rich and very interesting; but first we'll delve into a brief overview of their origins. They are thought to have moved from Northern Mexico, eventually settling in the city of Tenochtitlan after a long and treacherous journey through Mexico.

Although the Aztecs had a different theory on how they eventually settled in Tenochtitlan, historians and archaeologists alike believe that they began their journey sometime in 1100. It's thought that they settled down in the city of Tenochtitlan in 1325; journeying for many years until they eventually found the place, they could call home.

It is also thought that they attempted to settle down many times before this but were continuously pushed out, often facing conflict with nearby cities and thus continued to wander Mexico until they came to reside in what would one become the Aztec empire known as Tenochtitlan.

Aztec legends say that the priests stopped the Aztecs from moving forward, as they were given a sign that they were meant to settle in Tenochtitlan.

Jarus, O. (2017, Online) explained that:

"...Huitzilopochtli, the god of war, the sun and human sacrifice, is said to have directed the Mexica [Aztecs] to settle on the island. He "ordered his priests to look for the prickly pear cactus and build a temple in his honor. They followed the order and found the place on an island in the middle of the lake ..." writes University of Madrid anthropologist Jose Luis de Rojas..."

Once the Aztecs had settled, they set about building a place that they could call home, they worked hard to study the layout of the land and how exactly they could thrive in such a strange environment. By 1350, they had begun to build canals and causeways around their settlement, making it far more liveable than it was when they first arrived and putting the groundwork in to help it blossom into a city. Gradually, from those years of hard work, it started to become something more.

By 1375, the Aztecs had established a beautiful, thriving society that they could call home. They decided however, to have someone to speak for them and continue to lead them into prosperity. As such, a man known as Acamapichtli came into power, to rule over them and continue to oversee the city, becoming their very first emperor. It was believed that the emperor had ties to the gods themselves, as such he was seen as wise and only to be rivalled by the gods.

Following the above, over the years the Aztecs continued to have many different leaders/emperors, each leaving their own mark and helping the city grow more and more. In

1427 Itzcoatl became their fourth ruler and from there Tenochtitlan grew into an empire.

Over the next year, the Aztecs expertly dove into politics, they formed alliances and began to expand their city further. By 1428 they had built what was known as the Aztec Empire with The Texcocans and the Tacubans by their side. They then used these alliances to defeat their enemies; the Tepanecs.

With their enemies defeated, the Aztec Empire only grew; in 1440 Montezuma I became their fifth leader and began to expand it. The small settlement blossomed into something grand; it was a truly something to behold as it was slowly becoming the biggest society in Mexico of that era.

Between 1440 – 1519 the Aztec empire had become the biggest in the world and in many ways; in what was considered by experts far ahead of its time. It was over *80,000* square miles throughout Mexico with a believed population of around 400,000 people. However, Montezuma was mostly to credit for this, as he ensured that it the empire was able to expand, and he continued to navigate the intricacies of the politics that came with such an expansion with expertise and diplomacy.

By 1487 the Aztecs had also notably finished their temple to be able to practise their faith and worship – notably called the Great Temple of Tenochtitlan; and they dedicated it to the Gods. From there they were able to begin their rituals and properly honour the gods (if you have heard of Aztecs previously in schoolbooks, or other such places then you may have heard about human sacrifice).

The Aztecs considered human sacrifices as part of their worship, and as such once the temple was built, that is where they begun making human sacrifices to the gods. They had achieved what they set out to do; and as they believed the gods created them, they sacrificed both animals and humans to appease and nourish them.

Eventually, Montezuma I's reign ended, and Montezuma II became the next ruler of the Aztecs; becoming the ninth leader of their empire in 1502. Unfortunately, in 1517 the Aztecs then sighted a comet in the night sky – the priests at the time deduced that this was a sign that they were doomed, and something was coming to bring their mighty empire down – and they were not mistaken.

Sure enough, only two years later in 1519, Montezuma II was captured after the Aztecs greeted Hernan Cortes in Tenochtitlan; they treated him as an honoured guest but then drove him from the city when he captured the emperor. Montezuma II was then killed in the crossfire as the Aztecs attempted to rescue their emperor, and thus they were forced to turn to the next in line for the royal throne.

Cuauhtémoc then became the last leader of the Aztecs in 1520. Yet, little did he know at the start of his rule that Cortes built an alliance with Tlaxcala – another of the Aztecs enemies – and he began to attack the Aztecs. He managed to concur the city, and by 1522 the Spanish had taken over the Aztec empire, leaving the Aztecs to disappear into the remainder of history.

The Spanish were displeased with the Aztecs and also with the rise of Christianity, when they conquered them, they set about destroying anything of the Aztec's culture that they could. Notably; they considered the Aztecs human sacrifices as barbaric and believed it to be pagan beliefs/devil worshipping and tried to wipe the Aztec influence from the city.

Over time, historians were able to obtain and collect what had remained of the Aztecs and some of their traditions were reincorporated into modern-day Mexican culture. However, even today historians and archaeologists alike are still learning things about Aztec culture as more is uncovered about this lost civilisation.

For a briefer timeline with dates, please refer to the appendix (Appendix A) where this can be found.

Where did they come from?

There are a lot of different theories on where the Aztecs originated from, however many believe that they came from the north of Mexico. Adams, S in Reasons for the Fall of the Aztec Empire (2011, p.g.4) explains that according to a well-known legend, they came from "Aztlan", a city that was in the northwest of the country.

It's believed that before they travelled and settled in Tenochtitlan, they were a small tribe that fished and hunted, yet they travelled as far as they did as they wanted a settlement that they felt was better able to appease the

Gods. In their current city of Aztlan, they did not have the means to worship the gods.

A lot of people, however, feel that the Aztecs came out of nowhere – whilst it is widely discussed and agreed upon that they came from the North of Mexico; nobody is sure exactly where.

The Aztecs themselves believed that they came from the city of "Aztlan" however, and they were brought to Tenochtitlan by one of their gods on a perilous journey. It was only after fighting various different societies, and killing the son of a goddess that they were able to settle in the city and build up their once great empire.

Society

Something which all scholars alike can agree upon is that the Aztecs had a thriving society; the likes of which are unrivalled throughout most of history. Their empire and the way that they managed society is incredible in a variety of different ways and they are considered ahead of their time.

They had developed their own structures and hierarchy. Some citizens were classified as being nobles and others commoners – all of which had set hierarchies of their own. For example, a peasant and a slave were very different from one another. In addition to this, nobles were anything from royals to landlords and had more privilege compared to the commoners, such as receiving gifts or tributes from the commoners.

Much like royalty, your blood also determined where you ended up in society itself; for example, if you were born into a noble family, you would stay within that circle. However, if you were born into a commoner family you would most likely not move above that – yet all children in the Aztec world were required to attend school; which was very different from other ancient civilisations.

All parents in Aztec society would also be penalised if their children did not attend school; education was mandatory in the Aztec empire and free to all to attend.

Interestingly enough, the society was also divided into various different groups; reflecting that of a pyramid. Carrasco, D. and Sessions, S. (2011, p.g.4) accurately depicts this;

> "...Their peoples were organized into a *social* pyramid, with masses of agricultural workers and commoner families forming the economic base of society. This widely distributed group supported a smaller number of merchants, warriors, and priests who formed the narrower middle section of society. At the apex of this society was a still smaller but nevertheless sizable group of nobles, high-level warriors, artists, priests and especially the ruler and his entourage. This pyramidal image also helps us understand the ceremonial character of society, for the larger Aztec communities were organized around impressive ceremonial centres dominated by a sizable pyramid temple..."

In other words, it reflected modern societies in some ways with a set working class, middle class and higher class; but each with individual characteristics and intricacies.

Ducksters (Online, 2019) summarises each one of the social classes; there were the Tecuhtli, the Pipiltin, the Pochteca, the Macehualtin and the slaves.

The slaves were at the bottom of the Aztec society – yet, if the slaves had children these would not be forced into slavery as well (as you may recall, children were required to attend school). People who became slaves would chose to do so for various reasons – such as repayments or even to serve out a crime sentence. Moreover, even though they were considered as the bottom rung of society the Aztecs ensured they still had basic rights and freedoms – one example being that unless they agreed upon it, they could not be sold.

Above the salves were the Macehualtin – these were the common people – which could also be compared to the working class of today. They all had professions and helped the Aztec society itself work as a whole, as it included farmers, craftsman and even warriors (although, it should be noted that some of the warriors were seen as a higher social standing than the farmers). Even though they had a lower social standing; these people were needed to make sure that the Aztecs could thrive.

Following the Macehualtin, there were the Pochteca. The Pochteca were merchants and were treated like nobles – although they were not of the noble class. They could be interpreted as the lower-middle class; as they had some of the same privileges as that of the nobles. These people travelled to bring goods and wares to the nobles themselves; and were a very important part of the Aztec society.

After the Pochteca there were the Pipiltin; these were also known as the noble class. They wore clothes and jewellery that highlighted their positions such as feathers and gold. The classes below them were not permitted to wear such things, as such all were able to be notified of their position by glancing upon their wears. These people were often priests, warriors or helped to rule the various parts of the Aztec society; yet they all had various high-ranking positions within society.

Finally, there was the Tecuhtli – these ruled the individual states/cities that made up the Aztec kingdom and lived in glamorous castles and palaces. As long as they paid tribute to the emperor that oversaw the whole of the Aztec cities that made up Tenochtitlan, they had the power to operate however they wished. The only other class that were above this one was the emperor himself.

However, there was one thing that that the Aztecs saw as sacred beyond anything else, which was marriage. Aztecs viewed family as one of the most important things within their society, and as such marriage was the lifeline of this. In particular, men could often have multiple wives; yet there was only a single woman that would run the household.

As the family unit was considered sacred, they often belonged to a larger unit that owned the land and operated like a smaller community within the Aztec society. The group of people that ran this were known as the Calpulli.

The Calpulli had local schools and all of them had a trade which they specialized in, they also had a leader that would act as a chief and make decisions for the rest of them – yet they all obeyed the emperor and operated under their instructions.

Politics

The politics during the time of the Aztecs were quite diverse and the Aztecs navigated them with intricate levels of wit and caution. They had many enemies – as any growing, wealthy empire would – but also had many allies to turn to for invasions or battles.

In some ways, the Aztec empire operated like America; it was made up of various states with officials that led them. These states were called the Altepetl and each one had a supreme leader, judge and administrator that would handle the day-to-day affairs of each state.

Collections, S. (Online, n.d.) breaks down how exactly the political structure was able to run so smoothly. The supreme ruler, who ruled under the state would oversee the various things that came with managing a state day-to-day. For example, they would manage the markets, receive tributes from those living in the state, would help manage the temples, would resolve any disputes that would come about and lastly they would lead the army/military powers in the state.

Intriguingly, the supreme ruler of the state would rule it for life; they were also considered to be seen as noble and royal lineage – which linked them to the emperor and therefore the gods. Following the supreme leader, should anything happen to them, the judge would be the second in command, and instead manage the state. They also would recruit court officials, and they handled the finances of the state.

Following the above, there was the emperor which oversaw the kingdom as a whole. The emperor had to be of royal blood and when one passed away, a high council of four noblemen (who were related to the ruler) would choose the next in line for the throne. Men were permitted to rule; so as such the following ruler when the emperor passed would be either a son or brother of the deceased that the high council would deem as worthy.

Whoever the emperor was, they were required to meet certain rules set about; such as being over thirty years of age, educated, warriors and they needed to be both just and fair in the eyes of the kingdom. Although the emperor was given these requirements, they did not make any decisions for the kingdom alone and they were entrusted with advisors that assisted them with the running of the empire.

Although the Aztecs were a glorious and thriving empire on their own, they also had an alliance to overthrow a mutual enemy. When the Aztecs settled in Tenochtitlan, a way in which their economic status began to thrive was by defending other societies. In particular, the Tepanec.

The Aztecs were gifted in trade and fighting, so before they were able to begin to grow their trade empire, they became warriors for the Tepanec and fought for them. In turn they were rewarded and so they were able to afford to begin growing things and learn more about the practises of agriculture.

However, the Tepanec often demanded tributes whenever the Aztecs fought for them and as the Aztec's society grew, so did the Tepanec's demands. As such, a steady conflict began to arise and that was where the Aztecs began to form an alliance. They grew tired that the Tepanec's were steadily demanding more and more from them, even though the Aztec empire was past the days of fighting and their empire in trade and agriculture was thriving. So, they decided to seek out alliances to be rid of the Tepanec once and for all.

As mentioned previously, Itzcoatl became the emperor of the Aztecs in 1427. Unhappy with the Tepanec, he began to form an alliance with the other two societies nearby during these ancient times to overthrow the them. He arranged to overthrow the Tepanec with the Texcocans and Tacubans.

Together, they created what is also referred to nowadays as the "Triple Alliance" and agreed they would fight side-by-side to put a stop to the Tepanec's once and for all. So, the alliance fought the Tepanec together and managed to defeat them, putting an end to their reign. Over time, this alliance also began to dominate any remaining societies that were nearby in Mexico and Tenochtitlan became the most powerful and modernized empire in all of Mexico.

Following their domination of the Tepanec and the surrounding societies, they gained control of large sections of Mexico and at it's height Tenochtitlan had a population that is estimated of around 250,000 people or more and the amount of land they had paled in comparison to that of Europe. However, as it began to expand because of the Aztecs conquests, they also began to gain more enemies.

The Aztecs wealth, domination and power made several nearby groups uneasy and their enemies grew more and more by the day. The Aztecs managed to largely remain in power due to their rulings, which entailed human sacrifices and payments.

There were those however, that hated the payments that the Aztecs would ask for. Paired with the human sacrifices, some of the societies turned elsewhere for aid and these small groups that felt oppressed and hated the Aztec rule eventually joined the Spanish when they launched their attack; helping bring this civilisation to an end once and for all.

Art

The Aztecs were well-known to be a fascinating society that were very artistic and cultural. As such, it is no surprise that there is still art that you can find today that is both inspired or that has survived that era.

Artisans and craftmanship were both seen as worthy professions; but they both were not seen as simply for cosmetic purposes. The Aztecs were very devout with their religious practises and this can be see throughout their works of art that were created in many forms; in temples, in music and in the legends that they told.

Aguilar-Moreno (2007, p.g.178) explains that in particular they used various objects that were perceived in their religion to show the power that the Aztec empire represented; they thought of themselves as mighty; they believed themselves to be created and led by the gods and as such it reflected parts of their everyday life.

Statues, pictures and pottery was made; but it was not made for any material purpose – instead, this was used to appease the gods and incorporate their admiration to them in their day-to-day lives.

The Aztecs beliefs were symbolized in various different ways, from serpents which represented the gods and the power they held, the eagle which showed strength of the warrior and the sun and even the shells which depicted the circle of life; creation, life and fertility. In fact; the Aztecs even used these things to show their own links to the gods – an example is that some high-ranking soldiers would often wear eagle feathers with their armour to show their bravery.

Moreover, Aguilar-Moreno goes on to explain that the Aztecs did not create art with the intention of it to be defined as art; instead they created it to serve a purpose – be it religion, war or even politics. Everything they made reflected a part of their society and day-to-day lives. Although art was appreciated, it served a much higher purpose than just to be admired. As such, statures or temples that were built served to worship the gods they followed rather than having another kind of purpose.

Artists of that era (also known as artisans) were therefore often jewellers instead. They would make fine jewellery that nobles would wear using crystals, silver and gold. A great deal of them would also use feathers to decorate fine clothing and goods. Nobles were often of a high ranking status and as the Aztecs depended mostly on dress to show their status, the artisans were prized for helping them be able to flaunt it better to the rest of the Aztec society.

Statues have mostly survived the time of the Aztecs and can be still found in museums today, but there is another form of art that exists to this day; poetry.

Poetry, like other forms of art in the Aztec world was linked to religion and the gods that they worshipped. It held a strong part in society and it was often performed by priests in various different ceremonies. Oftentimes, poetry would be sung or spoken dependent on what the priest preferred and it was one of the many art forms that children were taught as well.

Oftentimes, poetry was dedicated mostly to Quetzalcoatl who was believed to have bestowed the arts upon the Aztecs themselves.

Economy

As we have established previously, the society of the Aztecs was broken down into various different sections, with each one having intricate classes and a wealth and status system being clearly defined. Despite this, the economy was one that was unrivalled during it's time; and the Aztecs set up a society that was able to flourish and remain quite wealthy.

In other words, although the Aztecs had a hierarchy, they still brought in wealth to the society enough for it to thrive as a functioning economy, until they were overthrown by the Spanish and their enemies. Everyone in the society was able to eat and receive an education; no matter their social standing.

The Aztecs were able to obtain their wealth from various different methods. As discussed previously, they first operated as mercenaries when they arrived in Tenochtitlan, this allowed them to gain some wealth. Yet they invested what they earnt wisely, as they started looking into different ways they could bring money into their city.

Due to the above, over time they developed various other ways to bring in funds to the city such as trade and agriculture. We will delve more into the agriculture below, but for now we will look at the structured economy that they were able to set up as a result of their determination to become successful.

The farmers grew various vegetables, plants and other things that were popular and traded them accordingly. Some things include hemp, tomatoes, corn and even tobacco. This alone began to bring wealth in the city and with the help of merchants, they steadily set up markets that allowed them to trade various different wares.

In particular merchants and traders were an important part of the society and were seen as just below the noblemen –

slightly higher than the lower class. They would travel and trade and were respected throughout the empire for what they had to offer. Traders and merchants alike were able to go to different regions and sell things, or bring luxurious items into the city of Tenochtitlan, so over time they became a tool in helping the Aztecs succeed.

Of course, there were other forms of currency that existed, other than the method of trade. However, trading within the society made it what it was; an empire. The Aztecs ability to trade various wares and grow so much allowed them to grow.

Agriculture

Agriculture was one of the most important things within the Aztec Empire; it became the way that the Aztecs were able to be so successful and their wealth depended upon it. One of the reasons they were able to be so successful was because they were able to trade various products that they grew thanks to merchants and traders that often came into the city.

They grew a wide range of products (as mentioned previously), however, it is believed they grew mostly the following products:

- Hemp
- Maize/corn
- Beans
- Tomatoes
- Avocados

- Beans
- Squash
- Potatoes
- Turnips
- Chili
- Peanuts
- Limes
- Onions

There were many more, but based on the population that the Aztecs had at their peak it should come as no surprise that they were able to grow so much. The most popular thing that they grew was maize/corn; selling all the other kinds of foods that they grew or delivering them to the nobles to enjoy.

The World History Encyclopaedia (Online, n.d.) advised that there were two different groups of agricultural workers; labourers who managed the fields and planted crops, then the horticulturalists who had a more in-depth knowledge of the land. The horticulturalists would rotate the crops, manage the seeding and establish the when was best to plant or harvest their crops.

In addition to the above the above article goes on to say that the Aztecs had various different ways to utilize the farmland around them. They would use what was known as "Chinampas" to raise the ground around them, and use the natural flooding (or hand-make flooded areas) to grow things:

"Each chinampa field was remarkably similar in size and orientation. Measuring around 30 x 2.5 m, they were pegged out in marshy areas using long stakes. Each plot was bordered with a fence made of intertwined branches which, over time, became more solid as they collected mud and vegetation. The wall was further strengthened by the planting of willow trees at regular intervals. The planting area within the chinampa was filled with sediment and between each plot was a canal which gave access for canoes. The water was provided, and carefully controlled, by a combination of natural springs and artificial constructions such as aqueducts, dikes, dams, canals, reservoirs, and gates."

The method above was so popular and methodical that it can still be seen as used today in some places; many people still use this method to grow things.

In addition to this, this allowed the Aztecs to grow large amounts of food. At it's peak the Aztec empire had a huge population – unmatched by some countries even today. As such, they needed to make sure that they could grow a lot of food successfully.

Food and Drink

The Aztecs were very diverse in what they ate and drank; they were legendary in terms of agriculture, and as such they produced a great deal of different food and drinks to consume. Although, it was known that only the royals were able to overindulge themselves with the finest flavours and things that were grown throughout the empire.

Due to the above, royalty and other classes ate more refined food then those of the lower classes. Cutright, R. E. (2021, p.g.138 - 139) advises that the commoners often ate tortillas which they would flavour with various vegetables such as tomatoes. To ensure that their diet remained balanced and they still obtained protein from their meals, they would often add insects or small animals to the tortillas. The tortillas were also often made from the maize/corn that they farmed – whereas the other foods were saved for the noblemen or royalty.

Those who were considered noblemen or royalty were able to enjoy more extravagant flavours that their kingdom was able to provide. Not only could they enjoy the wide range of crops that the lower classes grew, but they also were able to enjoy more meatier dishes with the added variation with spices and sauces. In addition to this, they often they would have exotic, imported ingredients that merchants would bring to them.

One thing which royalty, noblemen and warriors were able to enjoy rather than the common class were chocolate. In particular, they often roasted cocoa beans, crushed them, roasted them and would crush them up; afterwards mixing them with water and sweetening with various different other flavours to make a sweet drink. It was believed that chocolate was a gift from the gods; as such you could only enjoy it if you were of a certain social standing. As royalty and noblemen were often thought to be linked to the gods, they were able to enjoy the sweet treat.

Religion

The Aztecs religious practises were very different to that of todays religions and ceremonies. They worshipped various different deities that were both male and female and each of them had a different purpose in the eyes of Aztecs. In particular, the Aztecs were known to participate in human sacrifices, which they would do to appease the gods and nourish them; we will look at this more in depth later in the book.

However, even with the ceremonies, religion was a very important part of the Aztecs day-to-day lives and it was incorporated in everything that they did. The priests that governed the temples within the Tenochtitlan were seen as one of the highest of the noblemen, and were often thought to be linked to the gods themselves. As a result of their religion, the Aztecs celebrated festivals throughout the course of the year, often one each month that corresponded with a certain god or goddess each time.

As such, religion was such a huge part of society – and it is important to note that although priests were often see as godly, there were various other practitioners that would operate within the society in the eyes of the gods and goddess that the Aztecs used to ensure that they worshipped correctly. Some examples include monks, nuns and even priestesses; there were even other forms religious specialists – a good example of this is that in the military they often incorporated priests into their planning; determining when the best time to attack was or go into battle.

Chapter Two
Aztec Philosophy, cosmology and Legends of creation

Values

Aztec philosophy has always been seen as highly valued and different to most other societies around their time – in some ways it has even been seen as ahead of it's time because of how different it was to many others and the modern values that it seemed to incorporate. In particular, Aztec philosophers believed that morality and balance was essential for living a good life – which in turn would provide stability to an ever-changing world. The Aztecs felt that balance was necessary in everything that we did as a whole; the gods modelled balance and as people they thought that we too needed to find balance in our lives.

A lot of the Aztec legends symbolise the above, as in many of the legends the gods sacrifice themselves to stabilise the world and ensure that it could turn and allow life to thrive. As such, Aztecs thought that just as the gods needed to stabilize the world; we needed to ensure that we had the right amount of balance in our lives to stabilise our souls and existence.

Blog Contributor (Online, 2017) further explained this by advising that the Aztec people believed they had to find balance internally. In particular they explain that the Aztec people believed that everyone should seek balance between their desires and judgement of themselves. By being able to achieve both, a person would be considered as someone that could live a fulfilled and fruitful life.

The above article also goes on to advise that the Aztecs believed that everyone was prone to making mistakes and that because of this, life could be full of turmoil and struggle – so in many ways it was pointless to wallow on such a thing; in other words, life was already full of misery, so why waste time thinking more on it?

However, despite this, the Aztecs main view of life was that it was still worth living – no matter how many mistakes you made, or how rough the world would get - as long as you still ensured there was enough balance in your life to make it a worthwhile one.

Moreover, the Aztecs believed that you should care for your body just as much as you cared for your mind. Having both a healthy body and mind was essential in making sure that you lived a balanced and fruitful life. The above article goes on to advise that:

> "we know that the Aztecs urged a daily regimen of bodily activities that closely resemble yoga practices: stretching and strengthening exercises. This was one of the ways, at least, that one was to take root in one's body."

As such, the body, mind and heart were all seen as sacred in the eyes of the Aztecs; to achieve true balance, they believed that you needed to look after every element of it and only then would you be happy.

Reality

Interestingly enough, Aztecs all held a belief and an idea about the way that reality itself was structured. They believed that reality was fluid in a way; that time itself was in process and ongoing – which is why (as well as keeping track of when to celebrate the gods) they kept calendars. As such, this meant that it was even more important to lead a life worth living, as the Aztecs believed that time was always in motion and as such, every moment of it should be valued accordingly.

Although they had quite interesting beliefs on the concepts of time and reality, they did hold very rigorous religious beliefs in how it had been shaped and the world had came to be what it was.

They believed that our reality was structured by the gods; in particular they believed that the world itself lived on the back of a sea-monster that the gods had torn apart to create the world. Yet, despite this they still believed that time itself, and as such, the world was constantly moving forwards, transforming and evolving – and that it was impossible to change what was. In that respect, it's notable that they were very perceptive of time itself passing; they knew that it was ever in motion.

This is another reason why the Aztecs were thought to be more ahead of their time in comparison to many other ancient civilisations; they held many thoughts and concepts on how time, reality and their world was not only shaped but how it impacted their lives.

Cosmology

In modern times, we still look up at the stars and consider their meaning and what lies beyond what we can see in space. NASA for example, are forever expanding and sending ships to the stars and using telescopes to take incredible photographs and help us better understand what lies beyond earth itself.

We often ponder what the origin of the universe was and how it developed to get us to where we are – and because of this, we often wonder if there is life elsewhere and beyond what we can imagine. The stars themselves provide us with that constant wonder.

However, it should be noted that taking a keen interest in the sky above us is not new, and it is something that the Aztecs also took into consideration. Yet, the Aztecs incorporated the night sky into their beliefs and held the notion that it was just as significant as any other part of their lives.

In the eyes of the Aztecs, they believed that the world was split into a total of thirteen heavens, nine earth layers/the never regions. Wikipedia (Online, 2021) explains that:

> "The first heaven overlaps with the first terrestrial layer, so that heaven and the terrestrial layers meet at the surface of the Earth. Each level is associated with

a specific set of deities and astronomical objects. The most important celestial entities in Aztec religion are the Sun, the Moon, and the planet Venus (both as "morning star" and "evening star"). The Aztecs were popularly referred to as "people of the sun".

Many leading deities of the Aztecs are worshiped in the contemporary or present-day world."

Therefore, as the Aztecs believed themselves to be "people of the sun" they were concerned with the night sky.

Creation

The Aztecs believed in creators gods – and had many that they believed in. They believe that they came together to create the universe itself:

- Ometeotl; the Lord of Duality
- Quetzalcoatl
- Tezcatlipoca
- Xiuhtecuhtli
- Tlaloc

Although Ometeotl was seen as the main creator gods, the others each did their part to help create and organize the universe – and in turn the world itself – into what the Aztecs perceived it as now.

Ometeotl was believed to be the God of all things; it was the lord of duality and simply just was; it brought itself into creation. Before it created itself – there was nothing.

As the god of duality it was also neither male nor female –
it was thought to just be.

Once the above god created itself, it then created four
different gods, which later became the pinnacles of the
Aztec worship. Notably; the Aztecs didn't worship this god
– although it was technically the creator of the gods that
made the world, and the universe itself, it didn't interact
with anything beyond creating itself and the gods that then
created humankind.

As a result of the above, the Aztecs believed that the dual
god of duality existed beyond the world itself and thus
outside of the influence of the gods and humans alike. As
such, they felt it would be pointless to worship such a
being – as unlike the other gods it would not be able to
recognize or hear the prayers and worship that the people
could give.

Following the above, there were gods that were more
highly noted and regarded by the Aztecs. One in particular
was Tezcatlipoca who some Aztecs feared. He was seen as
intimidating and overbearing – as he represented darkness
and was thought to be everywhere at once.

Then there was Xiuhtecuhtli who was seen as a fire god –
who they believed that impacted society itself. The Aztecs
believed that he was the light of life in a lot of ways; he
would light up homes with his fire and temples would
often blossom with a flame in his image.

In particular, fire ceremonies and festivals would be used
to celebrate the gods. There was also the fire festival –

which was noted in the Aztec calendar – and it would be celebrated every 52 years.

Lastly, there was the creator god Tlaloc was seen as someone who was important on a day-to-day basis. He was thought to be the source of rain; that would nurture what the Aztecs grew. Like the other creator gods; Tlaloc was very important to the Aztecs; as agriculture allowed the Aztecs to be able to trade, and turn it into the wealthy society that it became.

Chapter Three
Aztec Patheon; Major Deities

Overview

As briefly mentioned above, there were many deities that the Aztecs worshipped, in particular there were some gods that were more prominent than others especially in legends, myths, rituals and ceremonies. However, it is also worth noting that the Aztecs had both Gods and Goddesses that they worshipped; with both providing different purposes to the Aztecs day-to-day lives.

Over the course of this chapter, we are going to review each god and goddess that the Aztecs worshipped and saw as part of their everyday lives; but only the main ones that were the most prominent in their culture (as there are hundreds and hundreds of Gods that the Aztecs worshipped, or would thank).

Huitzilopochtli

The Aztecs worshipped Huitzilopochtli, as he was believed to be the one who guided the Aztecs to their one true home and helped them create Tenochtitlan where they settled. As such, it is said that the Aztecs built the very first shrine to honour the God on the spot they believed that Huitzilopochtli said they should settle.

Due to the above, the Aztecs greatly worshipped this God; he was seen as the "father God" of all and he was seen as the maker of humankind. Highly revered and a friend to the Aztecs, he was one of the gods that the Aztecs sought consistent inspiration from.

In particular, the Aztecs ensured that he had a larger shrine in the empire once a temple had finished being constructed; although this shrine was decorated with skulls (which were from human sacrifices the Aztecs had delivered; believing that blood was the most powerful thing to aid the gods).

He was often depicted or symbolised as an eagle; as this was the God's spirit animal; just like the god the eagle was brave, valiant and resilient. Alternatively, he was likened to that of a hummingbird – as the legends said that the god was conceived when his mother fell pregnant with hummingbird feathers.

As a result of the above, it was believed that when soldiers passed during battle, or even those who were sacrificed in honour of Huitzilopochtli, would become hummingbirds; thus being reborn in the image of the god himself.

The god Huitzilopochtli also represented wars, which may have been why warriors were often thought to have been reincarnated as the symbol of him as hummingbirds. As Huitzilopochtli was likened to a warrior god, many prestigious soldiers throughout the Aztec kingdom (as previously mentioned) would wear elaborate eagle feathers decorating their clothing to signify their bravery in battle, their status and their connection to the god.

Most importantly however, was that this God was one of which that would need human sacrifices to continue to survive and help the sun continue to cross through the sky. As such sacrifices would often be made in his honour accordingly throughout the year to ensure that the god would be able to aid the final sun. The Aztecs believed that if you were chosen to be sacrificed it was one of the highest honours; as your blood was helping to fuel the gods (blood was believed to be a form of nourishment).

As Huitzilopochtli assisted the sun in it's journey, the Aztecs believed that he was constantly fighting the gods of darkness – and as such human sacrifices were made so that he would receive the appropriate nourishment to continue fighting them without fail.

As Huitzilopochtli needed plenty of power to continue fighting his war against the darkness; the Aztecs would sacrifice slaves and captives that they held, rather than other members of society. However, even if you were held as a captive or a slave; in the eyes of the Aztecs it was still a high honour to be sacrificed to the gods to nourish them.

The Aztecs also celebrated Huitzilopochtli in various festivals throughout the year. However, the most well-known one was the "raising of flags" celebration that lasted throughout December. This celebration would celebrate the Aztecs journey with Huitzilopochtli from Aztlan to their new home in Tenochtitlan.

Due to Huitzilopochtli's natural fighting prowess (he was believed to have been born in battle gear!) he is also believed to have another influence on the Aztecs; often being seen as an inspiration for battle. As such, war was seen as highly valued; the Aztecs were well-known for their wars (and the one that led to their demise).

Lastly, the god was believed to be joined by a select number of people upon death. The Aztecs would believe that the spirits of warriors, or women who died during childbirth would join him – spending a year aiding him in helping the sun with it's journey across the sky before becoming immortalized as hummingbirds.

Tonatiuh

Tonatiuh was the fifth and final sun, coming from the God's sacrifice of Nanahuatzin who threw himself into a fire to be able to nourish the world. He became the god Tonatiuh after leaping into the flames. However, Tonatiuh was a sun god deity that wasn't as strong as the other suns, and as such he struggled to turn across the sky.

As such, just like just like Huitzilopochtli he required some form of sacrifice, so the gods had to drain some of their blood to assist Tonatiuh in his journey across the sky. Due to this, the Aztecs believed the sun god also required human sacrifices and their blood, as he needed this nourishment. The Aztecs further believed that by human sacrifices Tonatiuh was able to provide warmth to the Aztecs via the sun, which was an important tool in ensuring they could continue to grow the many things that helped them create an empire.

Warriors often were linked to Tonatiuh, as they would ensure that he had many human sacrifices they could give. The warriors would also said to, when they died, accompany Tonatiuh's journey across the sky. The sacrifices were often chosen by soldiers themselves and they would both drain blood or sacrifice human hearts to assist Tonatiuh.

Of course, Huitzilopochtli was the most renown/prominent God in Aztec culture; Tonatiuh's great sacrifice meant that they could have daylight. As such, he fought against darkness on a daily basis and as such, the Aztecs believed that he required more regular sacrifices so that he would never be defeated – and so that he would continue to shine.

Xipe Totec

Xipe Totec was another important god in the eyes of the Aztecs as he provided food for humankind. As such, he was believed to be the god of agriculture and fertility. Like the other gods, he would usually be offered human sacrifices as tribute.

The Aztecs believed that Xipe Totec flayed himself, stripping his skin to be able to feed humanity. He stripped his skin like corn loses its outer layer before sprouting; and was thought to be compared to that. Some seeds strip their outer layer to germinate and the god had done something similar in order to feed humanity.

Due to this, there were many rituals surrounding this god; there was usually a ceremony to worship him in spring. The Aztecs would usually use a war criminal or prisoner, then kill them by removing their hearts. Following this, their skin would be peeled off and an Aztec priest would wear it.

Young warriors often would bring their captured prisoners as a right of passage to move further within the military as well for this ceremony. As such, Xipe Totec held an important place in a warrior's eyes, as he also signified the start of their battle journeys.

The Aztec priests would wear this skin for twenty days throughout the spring festival then discard it at the end; signifying Xipe Totec's shedding of his own skin to give new life.

Of course, it is not a surprise that the Aztecs relied heavily on sacrifices as they considered this the highest form of tribute and power; human blood was seen as nourishment to the gods.

Coatlicue

Coatlicue was a goddess whose name loosely translates to "serpent skirt" or "skirts of serpents" and was seen as a mother goddess. She was seen as the goddess of fertility and often thought to be linked to the earth. She was often referred to as the "skirts of serpents" as it was thought she wore a skirt full of writhing snakes.

She was also believed to have birthed Huitzilopochtli who was seen as the main god of worship by the Aztecs. As it was believed that she created Huitzilopochtli, she was often also seen as the goddess of childbirth; and was often seen as ferocious and strong because of it.

Due to her strong and resilient nature, she was also associated with warfare; the fact that she was compared to fertility also meant that the Aztecs often praised her for their success in agriculture as well.

Coatlicue was also said to have given birth to 401 sons (including Huitzilopochtli) and a daughter. As such it was believed that her chest hung heavy from having to nourish so many children.

In addition to the above, the Aztecs believed that she created the stars and the moon in the sky. Although she was admired by the Aztecs, they also greatly feared her. Like the other gods, she also needed nourishment of human blood – so human sacrifices were also common.

Quetzalcoatl

This god was perceived to be a symbol of death and resurrection, he also had his companion Xolotl and together they helped create mankind.

It was believed that he was responsible for many things within creation; one example being humans. The Aztecs believed that he created them by collecting bones from the underground, then mixed them with his blood; and thus the first humans were born.

However, the tale itself on how he was able to obtain the bones from the underworld is quite the story. Mythopedia (online, n.d.) advises:

> "Quetzalcoatl had to sneak into the underworld of Mictlan and trick Mictlantecuhtli and Mictecacihuatl, the Lord and Lady of Death, into giving him the bones they guarded. Mictlantecuhtli would only give the bones to Quetzalcoatl if he could create a sound by blowing into a conch shell with no holes in it. Quetzalcoatl managed to complete this challenge through clever trickery. He had worms drill a hole in the conch, then filled the shell with bees. Quetzalcoatl's actions successfully tricked Mictlantecuhtli into giving him the bones. But this was not enough for Quetzalcoatl. In an effort to further trick Mictlantecuhtli, Quetzalcoatl told him that he would leave Mictlan without the bones.
>
> Before Quetzalcoatl could escape from Mictlan, however, his deception was discovered by Mictlanecuhtli. A deep pit appeared before Quetzalcoatl, preventing his escape. As he fell into the pit, Quetzalcoatl was knocked unconscious and mixed up the bones he was carrying. After his eventual escape, Quetzalcoatl combined the now slightly shuffled bones with his blood and corn to create the first humans of the fifth age.6 The Aztecs used this allegory to explain why people came in all different heights."

This god was also believed to represent intelligence, wind, rain and self-reflection. In addition to this, the Aztecs also believed that he invented calendars and books. As he was known as an intellectual God, he was often featured in schools for children of nobles, where they would learn various different things such as war, astrology and the history of the Aztecs and the other Gods they worshipped.

Tezcatlipoca

This god was Quetzalcoatl's brother and the more unpleasant legends often speak of how often they fought (one example being that he Tezcatlipoca drugged him and drunkenly Quetzalcoatl slept with his sister – he ended up being so embarrassed that he fled).

The Aztecs often celebrated this god, in particular there was Toxcatl ceremony celebrated throughout May. The festival often featured a man who was treated as if he was the god himself throughout most of the year, then in May he was sacrificed.

The man who was chosen was often a slave that was selected, following this they were bathed and treated like the god himself for the year until May fell. He would wear expensive jewellery, would be worshipped by all around him and have great feasts in his honour. During the last month before he was sacrificed, the man would then be married to four women and finally, he would be dressed in warrior attire and sacrificed. It was considered however, like other sacrifices in the name of the gods, to be a great honour to be sacrificed.

This god was known as both a mighty creator and destroyer; like many other parts of Aztec society he was god of duality – as the Aztecs believed prominently in the cycle of death and rebirth. It was believed that he fought with his brother repeatedly to gain control of the world; during the first age he became a jaguar and destroyed the world due to his brother attempting to hurt him. In the second age that his brother created, he overthrew his brother – to which his brother turned the people into monkeys. In the third age, Tezcatlipoca stole Tlaloc's wife (who was the third sun at the time), to which Tlaloc responded by making it rain fire. Then, on the fourth sun Tezcatlipoca made fun of the god who was in the sky – causing the sun to cry and create great flood.

Although he was certainly terrifying – given his destructive ways with his brother, the kings and young warriors often worshipped him and paid tribute. In particular, people were often frightened of this god; as he was often depicted to smite people. The Aztecs believed that just as giving as Tezcatlipoca could be – as he was one of the many gods who put the creation of mankind in motion – he could also take things away too should he wish to do so.

Tlaloc

As mentioned previously, Tlaloc was often viewed as another creator god; the Aztecs believed that he provided the rain that was much needed for the Aztecs to sustain their crops and ensure they continued to be the prominent trading empire they are.

Although he was seen as someone who provided rain, that was life-giving, he was also feared in some ways as well. It was thought that he could be destructive and could make floods, storms and even droughts – an example of this is that he made it rain fire destroying one of the earth's cycles. As such, the Aztecs ensured he had a main shrine in the centre of Tenochtitlan in their temple, beside Huitzilopochtli's and ensured that they honoured him to the best of their ability to keep him appeased.

People were also said to have feared him as it was believed that he could also make hurricanes, lightening or diseases such as leprosy. As such, he was greatly feared – yet, although it was said he caused such things, the Aztecs believed that if you died from one of the above then Tlaloc would allow you to live in the paradise that he lived in, a huge, beautiful garden forever.

As with the other gods Tlaloc also needed human sacrifices to continue to remain powerful. For Tlaloc however, they sacrificed children rather than adults. Priests would pull out children's hearts and offer them to the God Tlaloc, it was also believed that the if the children cried before they were sacrificed, then the Aztecs would be blessed with heavy rainfall to be able to sustain their crops – in other words, the more tears, the better in the eyes of the Aztec priests.

Chalchiuhtlicue

Like the other gods, the goddess Chalchiuhtlicue was seen as both a giver of life and a deity to be feared. The Aztecs believed that she could take away things just as easily as she could provide something in abundance. A good example of this is that during her time as the sun, she cried and created many floods that killed mankind at the time.

Read, K. A. and Gonzalex, J. J. (2002, p.g. 142) goes on to explain the above, by advising that:

"Like her various waters, Chalchiuhtlicue appeared in both positive and negative forms. She could provide the waters necessary for growing crops, in which case, she associated with a young virgin the corn goddess Xilonen; or if she chose to withhold her moist bounty, drying the earth and killing the crops, then she associated with the slavering snake goddess Chicomecoatl. Like many water deities, Chalchiuhtlicue often appeared with Quetzalcoatl who, as the wind, moved the waters. Certainly the wind helped churn the waters into a dangerous place for boaters, but Chalchiuhtlicue also could act alone, stirring herself up into whirlpools and great waves that dangerously swallowed or rocked hapless vessels."

This particular goddess is believed to be the wife or sister of Tlaloc and also represents the life-giving water that the Aztecs needed.

In addition to the above, the Aztecs believed that Chalchiuhtlicue made certain waters have healing powers. Of course; water was seen as life giving and because her water was believed to be so powerful, the Aztecs believed that they owed her a great debt.

As such, the Aztecs would make human sacrifices to help sustain her, and repay her for the life-giving waters that she was able to provide.

Chapter Four
Lesser Known Deities

Overview

The Aztecs worshipped many Gods; but below are some of the lesser known ones that are believed to still have played an interesting part in Aztec culture.

Ahuiateteo

Ahuiateteo was made up of five different gods; and this term grouped them together. These gods were seen as the gods of pleasure. These gods were also linked with the South (as the gods were often split into various different sections North/East/South/West).

Each god was meant to show that gluttony, greed and excessive pleasure could often lead to decay – and as such was often associated with vices such as gambling, sex and drinking.

These gods are:

- Macuilcozcacuauhtli

- Macuilcuetzpalin

- Macuilmalinalli

- Macuiltochtli

- Macuilxochitl

Macuilcozcacuauhtli was seen as the god of excessive eating – in other words gluttony. All of the gods in the Ahuiateteo were meant to represent that it was important not to do something excessively, such as eating. He was often represented as a vulture as well in most ancient texts and in the mythology.

Macuilxochitl on the other hand represented both music and gambling. The Aztecs thoroughly believed that balance was important and this translated well to these Gods; by doing something in excess – you were not fully balancing your heart, body and mind.

The next God we will review is Macuiltochtli which was the god of alcohol – or drunkenness. Like a lot of other ancient civilisations, the Aztecs liked to drink; in particular a liquor known as octli (which they produced by fermenting sap).

Lastly, there were the two gods that were considered the gods of excess; Macuilmalinalli and Macuilcuetzpalin. These two were considered the gods of excess and over-indulgence (although, it is not significantly well known in what regard; only that they are portrayed as overindulging themselves). They are often likened to Gods as pleasure as well; which suggests that they were gods of excess with sex as well.

Cinteteo

It should come as no surprise that given how valuable agriculture was, that the Aztec had gods just for that purpose exactly. The Cinteteo was split into four different gods which each represented a certain kind of maize – which was one of the most popular foods during the reign of the Aztecs. Corn was seen as one of the things that was the easiest to grow and feed the masses. It was also central in them gaining the wealth that they had, and they regularly used it for trading purposes.

There were:

- Iztāc-Cinteōtl; which meant they looked over/ were the god of white corn.

- Yayauhca-Cinteōtl – who looked over black corn.

- Tlatlauhca-Cinteōtl which looked over red corn.

- Lastly, Cozauhca-Cinteōtl who looked over the Aztecs yellow corn.

All of these God's name represented that of which the corn they looked over.

Huehuecóyotl

Huehuecóyotl was another lesser god that you may not have heard of with the Aztec lore and was considered another of the less well-known deities.

This god was considered to be the lord of mischief and would often pull pranks to help relieve his boredom –

however, in most of the situations the Aztecs told of this god, his pranks would more often than not, backfire on himself.

In an article by Vickery, K. (Online, 2018) advises that:

"As all Aztec deities, Huehuecóyotl was dualistic in his exercise of good and evil. He was perceived as a balanced god; depictions of his dark side include a coyote appearance (non-human) with black or yellow feathers, as opposed to the customary green feathers.

In most depictions of Huehuecóyotl, he is followed by a human drummer, or groups of humans that appear to be friendly to him (as opposed to worshipping), which is exceptional in Mesoamerican culture.

Stories derived from the Codex Telleriano Remensis make him a benign prankster, whose tricks are often played on other gods or even humans but tended to backfire and cause more trouble for himself than for the intended victims. A great partygiver, he also was alleged to foment wars between humans to relieve his boredom. He is a part of the Tezcatlipoca (Smoky Mirror) family of the Mexica gods, and has their shape shifting powers.

Those who had indications of evil fates from other gods would sometimes appeal to Huehuecóyotl to mitigate or reverse their fate. Huehuecóyotl shares many characteristics with the trickster Coyote of the North American tribes, including storytelling and choral singing."

It was believed however, that even though he was cruel in his pranks and often seen as a god who enjoyed to party more than the others, he still brought gifts to humankind. As with the above, it was thought that he gave the ability for people to sing, dance and tell stories – thus bringing many forms of art into the world.

In addition to the above, he's often portrayed as a God who offers justice in an unforgiving world; as could be seen by above with some prisoners asking him Huehuecóyotl to undo their fate.

Chapter Five
Housing

As the Aztecs settled, they made houses that they could settle in for the reminder of their lives. However, the homes that people had and the extravagance of it varied depending on their social standing. An example is the emperor lived in a palace, whereas the peasants would live in far less glamorous housing.

Common Housing

Most commoners that lived in the Aztec times had a very simple house. The floor of the interior would be made from stone, or earth – dependent on where it was – and the walls were large mud bricks entwined with wooden strips and covered in plaster. The roof was either thatched or terraced and the simples houses would be divided into four different parts.

There would be the part of the house where the family would sleep, another to cook or make food, then a place to eat and lastly the fourth area would be decorated as a shrine to the gods. In addition to the above, the entire house itself was lit up with small flames, as torches would decorate the surfaces.

The shrine room was often the most prominent and families would use the shrine room to pray together.

In some common households however, the kitchen would not be in the house, instead it would be outside in the courtyard and they would share it with their neighbours.

In terms of bathing, common houses would not have anything luxurious to bath in, but instead as the Aztecs were quite hygienic and preferred to look after themselves to the best of their abilities. Every home was therefore equipped with a steam bath nearby in a separate building.

Tenochtitlan was very different from other societies with the above regard; Aztec doctors believed that one of the keys to staying healthy was to remain hygienic. As such, every citizen of the Aztec empire had a separate building to their home – and was given a steam bath inside of it.

Unsurprisingly, the lower class did not hold many possessions as they were not wealthy. However, they would have some furniture such as reed mats to sleep on, chests to store clothes and things on, and jugs, bowls and other such things to make food with.

Noble Homes

Noble homes often followed suit of the above class, but they would often be made out of more durable and better materials. In addition to this, the nobles had more possessions than the classes below them and as such their homes would often be quite elaborately decorated.

The houses themselves would be built out of stone and traditionally, the nobles would also have their houses built on a courtyard, so it was often surrounded by flowers, vegetable gardens – or even in some instances fountains. However, even though they often lived in a courtyard, they would still ensure they were near the centre of the city that they lived in.

Nobles were a very prominent part of society; as such, they needed to ensure that they could easily be found and were close to the cities where laws, festivals and other such things were held.

The homes of the nobles themselves were also slightly different to that of a commoner due to their roofs; the roof was either flat or peaked compared to the commoners homes. Due to their status they also had more furniture that was better compared to the commoners, they would have softer beds and their shrines would be more adequately decorated.

Interestingly enough, the nobles also at times had second floors – whereas this was something that commoners were not permitted to have. The inside of the house was often decorated in bright, lavish colours as well or they would have intricate murals painted on them.

Emperor Palaces

The emperor lived in a palace and he also had many different homes throughout Tenochtitlan. The main palace in which the emperor resided in was built of high elaborate and beautiful stones and painted with bright colours. The palace had many different rooms.

As the emperor oversaw the whole city of Tenochtitlan there were rooms to greet nobles, to talk to commoners, to speak with the high council. In addition to that there were also rooms that housed weapons, the palaces caretakers and even any visitors to the kingdom. It was truly a palace that showed the emperors great and vast wealth and also is believed to have housed many treasures.

The emperors throughout the Aztec reign was also known to have more than one wife. As such, there were many rooms for his wives to stay in accordingly.

Although it sounds like it may have just been the emperor and his many wives, historians and archaeologists believed that the palace was usually bustling with life and that there were a great deal of people helping run the day to day activities such as:

- Guards
- Slaves
- Artisans
- Cooks
- Servants
- Warriors
- Royal wives and the children of them
- Judges

Many people spent their day in the palace and as such, it was constantly busy. It was also believed that the palace had large courtyards, at least three – five, that you could wander through. In addition to this the palace was said to have had a pond, an aviary and even a zoo!

Chapter Six
Clothing

The Aztecs thrived in agriculture and growing things in the land, as such the majority of clothing was made of things that you could grow. As the city of Tenochtitlan was also quite hot, they would also wear light, durable clothing in most classes.

Common Wear

People who were deemed commoners, meant that they could had to wear appropriate clothing. Clothing was deemed to represent the class of someone; as well as jewellery. Oftentimes, this meant that the lower classes could not enjoy the comfortable, cotton garments that the upper classes would often wear. Instead, they would wear clothing that was made from agave plants or palm tree leaves. In turn, the women in the Aztec women of this class would take the materials and spin it into threads and weave together clothing.

In addition to the above, people of the lower classes within the Aztec kingdom were not permitted to wear feathers; as feathers depicted wealth and was something that the nobles could only enjoy. However, the material that they wove from the above plants was soft enough to be able to complete day-to-day tasks.

The slaves in particular would only wear very simple, basic clothing. Men would often wear loincloths that was either tied at the shoulder, or around the waist alongside a cloak. The cloak worked a bit like an apron and could either be used as clothing, or to store items in. The loincloth was called a Maxtlatl and the cloak that was adorned with it was known as a Tilmahtli.

Women wore something slightly different, and were permitted to wear skirts or a sleeveless bouse/shirt. The shirts were known as a Hupipilli, and the skirts known as the cueitl.

In addition to the above, both genders that were commoners or of the low social standing in the Aztec society were not allowed to wear shoes. They would have to go as barefoot for their day to day work and what not, as shoes were only see as something for higher classes. However, interestingly enough any kind of footwear was not allowed in a temple or in the presence of their leader/emperor.

Children of commoners often wore the same thing, their parents often made the clothes for them and they would wear whatever they had been given.

Merchants

Merchants were seen as slightly above the common class, and were in some ways a class of their own. As a result of that, although they often had very basic clothing, they were allowed to decorate it more; especially as they often received jewellery from the nobles that they traded with.

Due to their slightly elevated status, although they wore loincloths, they would often adorn it with embroidery and some other designs to show their elevated status, and this would separate them from the lower class.

In addition to the embroidery, the merchants would often also have a fringe on their loincloths, which the lower classes would not have. As such, it would've been easier to spot them and the differences were clear. There was also the fact that merchants clothing tended to be more colourful and bright; compared to the plain clothing of the lower classes.

However, even though they were allowed to wear more elaborate clothing than the lower class citizens of Tenochtitlan, they were not permitted to wear something as extravagant as the noble classes, as their status was still beneath them.

Nobles

The nobles, being one of the higher standing classes, were able to dress with far more extravagance than the other classes. They were permitted to wear cotton, which was more comfortable than the materials the lower classes used.

Although the nobles often wore loincloths and capes like the lower classes, the difference was striking and immediately noticeable. Their clothing would be beautifully decorated, with feathers, gold, jewels, crystals and even fur. Their clothing was also very bright and colourful; as such they stood out in the crowd and would immediately be spotted due to their clothing.

The women, also wore similar clothes to that of the lower classes; but they would also be noticed due to the extravagance of them and the materials. Like the men, the clothing would be made from cotton and it would be bright and colourful. They would also decorate them with gold and jewels, sometimes wearing many jewellery like rings, bracelets, arm bands and earrings.

The way that the noble class dressed was meant to attract attention in a lot of ways; it was meant to show that you were part of a higher standing class and easily recognized. As such, this would mean that in events or festivals they could be easily picked from a crowd as well.

Soldiers

Aztec soldiers and warriors had a very different dress from the other members of society in the times of the Aztec Empire. Notably, the Aztecs did not have a uniform like most modern-day armies, but like the rest of the society, soldiers could easily be spotted based on their dress.

Some warriors, that were more decorated then others and had fought many battles, wore leather helmets and body armour that was made from quilted cotton. Whereas warriors that were less experienced would wear tunics with their loincloths, only adding warpaints to their dress.

There were also warriors that were more senior that would have far more elaborate clothing; they would be permitted to decorate their outfits with feathers or animal skins; which you may note was a privilege that was only permitted to the upper classes.

Of course the soldiers were split into ranks, so based on what their rank was would also dictate on what they may have been permitted to wear.

As mentioned previously, a lot of soldiers and warriors worshipped various different gods and this their armour would represent the deities they worshipped accordingly.

Priests

Whilst priests were a form of nobles in a sense, they did have an elevated status from other nobles in a way – such as those who were leaders of the states that made up Tenochtitlan – as such, they wore very interesting attire.

Priests had a very set amount of clothing; most of them traditionally wore sleeveless jackets, or waistcoats. In addition to this, this clothing often had many open slits that they could use to accessorise it with jewels or feathers. This clothing was called xicolli.

In addition to the above, priests would also ensure that they wore a backpack, or something to carry items. Most priests would have on them a incense burner, incense and tobacco.

Although there were priests that led ceremonies there were also those that were needed for sacrificial purposes, and as such they wore different things. These priests traditionally wore more rough attire in comparison to the ones that would lead festivals.

Emperor

Royalty wore by far the most elegant and expensive attire in the Aztec kingdom compared to all others. Their clothes were lavish and one to be jealous of in a lot of ways. All of their clothes would be ornately decorated with jewels and they would often wear very colourful clothing as well.

Furthermore, the royalty would also have the royal symbol displayed somewhere on their clothing.

The emperor also wore a long, turquoise coloured cloak – that other members of the Aztec empire was not permitted to wear. Only the emperor was permitted to wear the cloak of this colour.

The main thing that the emperor wore that would make them stand out above all other members of the Aztec society however, was the headdress/crown. This was an ornate and unique thing that only the emperor was permitted to wear, that would show their position and standing.

Hairstyles

Surprisingly, just as much as clothing defined their statuses, the Aztec empire still had a basic number of hairstyles that all members of the society obliged to wear. Women often wore their hair in braids, that hung across the front of their face; and this often resembled two horns. At times, they would also mix herbs with their hair to dye it; purple was the most popular colour.

At times, women would often shave their head as well; it was not uncommon where a woman would have a completely shaved head if she wished to do so. For men, all men below the age of 10 had to shave their heads. As they grew older, the traditional hairstyle was to wear it short, and they would usually have it to their ears.

Finally, only the emperor was permitted to wear a headdress – and it was adorned with gold and feathers that were huge.

Chapter Seven
Medicine

The Aztecs – like in many other ways – were believed to be ahead of their time in terms of medicine. They had followed the advice of doctors throughout the empire and ensured that every home held a steam-bath. As such, the Aztecs were very clean people – they believed that every home should have a steam-bath and people should be able to bathe.

Medicine itself was interlinked with both religion and science. Although the Aztec doctors centred their beliefs around religion, they still used scientific methods to heal people and try and make them well in some instances.

Spiritual Medicine Practises

As mentioned previously in this book; the Aztecs believed that balance was essential in terms of getting healthy. In particular, they believed that as people we were divided into three spiritual parts as explained by Laack, I. (2019, p.g.98):

-   The heart (also known as the Toyollo/tonalli) which was what was perceived as the centre of affection, emotion and habit.

- The centre of the heart (also known as the Teyolia) which was the energy of the heart and relied on the eyes and ears – in particular, they believed that if you lost your teyolia you could die.
- The liver (known as the ihiyotl) this was where strong feelings laid and it was personality traits such as valliance. In particular, the Aztecs believed that if their ihiyotl became out of balance, this would lead to them feeling angry.

From the above, the Aztecs believed that all of them needed to work together so that you would be a happy and balanced person. If you any of them lost their balance, then you would become ill, angry or bitter.

Illness and Wounds

Although the doctors used the above spiritual practises, and would determine if someone was out of balance they would also rely on various herbs and plants for their research. Plants were often given to patients and following that the doctors would ask them to keep track of their symptoms to establish if it had any impact.

Over time, the Aztecs began to develop better ways to heal people the more they learned of various medical properties. However, they also used more traditional ways of healing some wounds or illnesses. An example of this was if warriors were injured on the battleground, they would pour boiling oil onto it to cauterize and close the wounds.

However, they did have a less than pleasurable mean of some as well; most wounds would be cleaned with urine, applying herbs, and then using sap. However, the kind of spa that the Aztecs used was later discovered in the 20th century to be thought of as an antibiotic. As such, it was thought that they were ahead of their time in the ways they seemed to know how to use certain substances for illnesses and wounds.

Magic and the Gods

The last way that someone might become ill was that they may be believed to have been punished by the gods. As mentioned previously in this book – sometimes upsetting certain gods could lead to you getting ill; such as if you didn't properly appease them or if you acted out of term. This could cause the gods to want to make you ill.

Aztec doctors also thought that enemies could make people ill with dark magic. They believed that if you fell ill with certain diseases, then this could be a result of someone casting a spell or a curse on you.

Ordinarily in both of the above situations, the doctors would see fit to fight magic with magic, and they would give the person who was ill an amulet or something else to ward off the curses they had been inflicted with.

Chapter Eight
Main Legends and Myths

The Aztecs had lots of rich lore in mythology and legends; for them it was a part of every day life. In particular, they believed the whole world around them reflected the gods and that everything they had was because of the gods sacrifices and wish to help humans to thrive.

The Sun

The Aztecs believed that darkness once reigned enteral, and that that was all that covered the world. Yet, there was a god that created itself; known as Ometecuhtli/Omecihuatl.

An article by Aztec History (Online, 2019) explains this in more depth:

> "Ometecuhtli/Omecihuatl, created itself. (Looking back, of course, the Aztecs believed that the many opposites that they saw in the world would have to somehow unite in the origin of the world.) This god was good and bad, chaos and order, male and female. Being male and female, it was able to have children. It had four, which came to represent the four

directions of north, south, east and west. The gods were Huizilopochtli (south), Quetzalcoatl (east), Tezcatlipoca (west), and Xipe Totec (north)."

Following the above, it was believed that the gods were able to create things; yet because the first thing they created was water they had a problem with an entity known as Cipactli. Cipactli devoured anything that the gods made, so a war was born.

From the war, the earth, heaven and hell was created. Notably, after this all the gods came together and made a fire. It was believed that from there, one of the gods then leapt into the flames and from there became the sun. The other gods then donated their blood, to help the sun blossom and from their the sun became truly alive and created life.

As a result of the above, sacrifice has always been believed to play a huge role in the religious worship of the gods in the eyes of the Aztecs. The Aztecs would follow suit of the gods by making human sacrifices, as mentioned previously, as they believed human blood would assist their gods.

Rebirth

The Aztec legends told that the earth had been reborn several times. They believed that it was a cycle; the gods themselves were not immortal either and would die over and over again, and be reborn. They saw it is a cycle in a lot of ways.

Death however, was not necessarily a bad thing in the eyes of the Aztecs; they believed that the world itself lived in continuous balance and as such death was balanced with life. In addition to this, they also believed that the gods would often sacrifice themselves for the sake of the greater good and to keep humanity itself afloat.

The rebirth of the world also foretold that it had happened several times. It was believed that it had happened four times before, but if it happened even once more – than it would be forever. In fact, the Aztecs believed that if this happened then their souls would be banished to the underworld forever and reach their interpretation of hell.

During the first age, they believed that the world ended because people died of starvation. In the second instance, they believed that it was destroyed by many winds. Then, in the third the world was destroyed by fire and the last one was water. As they were afraid of the world being destroyed once more, the Aztecs tried to ensure that the Gods had all the nourishment that they needed to make sure they could prevent the world from ending once more.

Several gods had sacrificed themselves to become the sunlight; and as such it's believed that the Aztecs modelled sacrifice after the gods. As the world had been reborn five times; the Aztecs believed that five gods sacrificed themselves to become the sun and that if it happened once more the earth would be thrown into turmoil with numerous earthquakes and it would destroy them all.

Origins of the Aztecs

Although the Aztecs are historically believed to have come from the north of Mexico, they personally believed that their god Huitzilopochtli came to them from their home Aztlan. The God was believed to have told them that Aztlan wasn't their real home and that this God would lead them to where they were meant to go.

In an article by Mesoweb (Online, N.D.) they translated the original story and record of what the Aztecs believed to be their origins. Following the above, the Aztecs followed Huitzilopochtli across the lands to where their true home would lie. Originally, the Aztecs apparently began their journey not just with Huitzilopochtli but also with Huitzilopochtli's sister – Malinalxoch. Yet, Huitzilopochtli was disappointed with her as it was believed she was a witch and caused people to do terrible things.

So, they continued on and away from the goddess until they stopped at the land known as Chapultepec. There, Huitzilopochtli told the Aztecs that Copil, Malinalxoch's son, would seek revenge for the Aztecs not allowing Malinalxoch to join them on their journey.

They fought Copil and managed to capture him. Huitzilopochtli advised that the Aztecs cut out his heart and they complied, then tossing it into a nearby lagoon and continuing onwards for their journey. As such, they went on until eventually they came upon the city of Culhuacan.

There they met with the chief of the lands and laid eyes upon her daughter, who they believed would be perfect for a new goddess; one who could become the symbol of fertile new growth. At the time, the chief did not quite understand and handed his daughter over to the Aztecs, who killed her, stripped her skin and put it on one of their priests.

For the ceremony of her to become a goddess, the chief joined the Aztecs and was horrified to find that his daughter had been killed and planned revenge on the Aztecs. A war began and the Aztecs were forced to go back to the lagoon and hide there.

When the Aztecs were hiding, Huitzilopochtli came back to them and told them to seek a cactus among the reeds, with an eagle on top. It was believed that this was where Copil heart had been thrown; as such it was where they would be able to build their city and concur their enemies once and for all.

Sure enough, they travelled through the lands until they found the symbol Huitzilopochtli had spoken of and settled there to found Tenochtitlan. It was also believed that the Aztecs had gone through a circle; much like the cycle of rebirth and death – they had started out on a small island, in a lagoon and that was where they had been told to settle by the gods.

Huitzilopochtli

Huitzilopochtli was quite popular with the Aztecs and was seen as a hero in some ways; mostly as he led the Aztecs to their home in Tenochtitlan. It should come as no surprise then that Huitzilopochtli's origins were seen as quite dramatic.

Huitzilopochtli's mother was the Coatlicue, and before she had Huitzilopochtli she had already bore 400 sons and a daughter. The myth of Huitzilopochtli states that Coatlicue became pregnant with him, as a floating ball of feathers fell on top of her.

The brothers and sister of Huitzilopochtli became angry that Coatlicue was pregnant yet again; as she already had many children. As such, they plotted against her and all agreed that she should be killed for her promiscuity. They felt embarrassed that their mother was still getting pregnant and in their eyes still having suitors, so they planned to murder her.

Despite not being born yet, Huitzilopochtli overheard his brothers and sister's plan and knew that he would protect his mother to the death. When Huitzilopochtli's brothers and sister were ready to slaughter Coatlicue, Huitzilopochtli was born. Yet, he was born as an adult, with armour and weapons. He fought all of his siblings and cut off his sister's head.

It was thought that when Huitzilopochtli cut off his sister's head he threw it into the sky and it became one of the moons to the stars.

The Rabbit Moon

There are two versions of this story, on how a rabbit helped to make the moon. The first is that of Quetzalcoatl; at one point he lived on earth, and did so as a human. Like many of the other gods in Aztec mythology, he could transform into a human to walk among it.

One time, he decided to wander the earth for quite a long time. Eventually, he became very tired with the hot sun pouring on him and no food or water in sight.

As a result of the above, he began to worry that he might die on earth. He settled down in the desert when a little rabbit approached him and asked him what was wrong. Quetzalcoatl explained that he was beginning to starve to death and the rabbit offered a carrot to the god.

He advised that the carrot that the rabbit was nibbling on would not provide enough sustenance for the god to continue on his journey. As such, the rabbit offered itself instead – advising that if Quetzalcoatl was to eat it then he would be able to survive.

Quetzalcoatl was touched by what the rabbit had offered and then transformed into his godly form again. He advised that the rabbit would always be remembered for it's noble sacrifice and as such lifted it to the moon to imprint it's image on there.

*

The other tale of the rabbit, comes from when the fifth and final sun was created by the Aztec gods. Nanahuatzin was the last god that had leapt into the sun to keep it burning for humankind and therefore became Tlaloc. However, there were two gods that tried to become the sun at that time.

The god Tecciztecatl was not well liked, but had agreed to become the fifth sun for humans, trying to remake the world after it had been destroyed four times before. However, when it came to the time to jump into the flames that would then go on to create the fifth sun, the god he said he would not. The Aztecs believed that he was frightened of the flames – he tried to jump in a few times but was so terrified from the heat and as such turned his back on them.

So, with the fate of the new world hanging in the balance, Nanahuatzin sacrificed himself to do so instead. Where Tecciztecatl would not jump, Nanahuatzin took his place and became the fifth sun in the sky to light up the day. The other gods were pleased; as Tecciztecatl was not very well liked anyway – and they praised Nanahuatzin sacrifice.

Tecciztecatl however, was embarrassed that he had not done what he was meant to and had let fear stop him. The god also became angry that Nanahuatzin had taken his place – and as such, he leapt into the flames as well. Due to his recklessness and hesitance, there were then two suns that shone in the skies.

The other gods were shocked; there were now two suns that both shone as bright as the other and they knew that humanity would not last if both shone as bright as one another.

Yet, they were all annoyed at Tecciztecatl for not hesitating and not jumping in as he should have; and only doing so after Nanahuatzin had jumped into the flames. As such, the gods threw a rabbit into the face of Tecciztecatl and as such, it dimmed the light of the second sun.

Eventually the second sun became so dim that it could only shine during the night; but would never rival that of the daylight sun.

Due to the above two stories, it is believed that if you inspect the moon close enough, you will be able to see the rabbit (which is believed to be from either story).

How Music Was Made

As with everything, the Aztecs also had a story and a way on how they believed music came into the world. They believed that Tezcatlipoca and Quetzalcoatl came together to create music.

In the world, there was once no music – the only sound was the gushing waves or the flowing wind, so together the two gods planned to take it from the sun. The house of the sun had all the musicians, so the earth had none at the time.

Quetzalcoatl spied on the island – the house of the sun – before commanding his servants to assist him to get there. Sure enough; the god's servants appeared and made a bridge to the island and searched for the musicians.

The god became lost, until he heard the sound of the music and followed it to where there were musicians, playing various instruments or singing. The sun saw that Quetzalcoatl was on the island and commanded that the musicians stopped playing, as it was fearful they would take the musicians away from the house of the sun.

The musicians instantly became silent, which made Quetzalcoatl angry. He began to create a large storm from his anger and the musicians flocked to him immediately fearful of his wrath.

Once the musicians had come to the god, his anger disappeared and Quetzalcoatl gathered the musicians, leaving the House of the Sun and climbed the bridge back to earth. Once the musicians arrived, flowers bloomed and new bright, deeper colours filled the land.

Eventually, from Quetzalcoatl's gathering of these musicians, people learned to sing – but music didn't stop there. Birds learnt to sing, the trees, the water and all things on earth were soon humming with a tune of life,. The musicians loved their new home and the Aztecs believed that since Quetzalcoatl brought them to earth, music has been present everywhere.

Chocolate

Chocolate is still consumed to this day, and has always been known of a sweet treat. However, the Aztecs believed that this gift was delivered to them by the gods – and that it was the gods that were able to give them the power to be able to create such a sweet flavour.

Morganelli, A. (2006, p.g.11) explains that Quetzalcoatl presented the Aztecs with the cacao seeds:

"According to the ancient Aztec Legend, a white-skinned, bearded god named Quetzalcoatl, the god of wisdom and knowledge, came from his land of gold to present the people with the seeds of the cacao tree. He taught them how to grow the cacao tree, to harvest its pods, and to prepare chocolatl..."

Following this gift, the Aztecs used chocolate as one of their more popular beverages – and as mentioned previously it was something that the nobles tended to enjoy. As a result of the above, it is also believed that the word chocolate is derived from the original Aztec word of "chocolatl".

*

Much like the tale of the rabbit and the moon there was another one for the legend of chocolate. It was believed that the sun god (a the time of this story, Xolotl) had hoarded and enjoyed the chocolate for himself – and was something only he wished to have, not wishing to share with the humans.

Xolotl at the time believed that only the gods should be allowed to have the cocoa beans; for they were the only ones who were worthy of enjoying such a thing. One day the wind god (Quetzalcoatl) stumbled upon Xolotl eating the cocoa beans. Xolotl shared the beans with Quetzalcoatl and following this Quetzalcoatl insisted that they share it with the people they created. He further insisted that it would be a great addition to all the other things that the Aztecs were already able to grow at the time.

However, Xolotl disagreed with this and believed that not everyone should be able to enjoy such a thing – he believed that the sweet treat should only be reserved for the gods. Insisting that there were some pleasures that humans were not meant to have.

Unhappy that the sun god was not willing to share chocolate with the people on earth, the wind god transformed himself into a blue frog and waited by the tree that grew the cocoa pods. Following this, it was believed that he began to sing and then the children of Tenochtitlan flocked to where the little blue frog was sitting.

The children were unequipped to be able to access the pods that held the cocoa beans, as such they went home and brought their parents back, who gathered and opened the pods. Following this, whenever the cocoa beans were harvested they would always leave some remaining for Quetzalcoatl who had been disguised as the blue frog and had taught them were to find chocolate.

Ironic in a way that following this myth, only the royals and noblemen ended up being the ones to enjoy the frothy, sweet treat! Although, it should be noted that whilst only royals were allowed to enjoy the treat – the Aztecs took this as a powerful lesson to always share what you have.

The Doomed Love

The Aztecs had a famous love story that is one to rival the popular tale of Romeo and Juliet! A tale of heartbreak and loss, this is the story of Popocatépetl and Iztaccíhuatl.

There are several different versions of the story, but the one thing that it all has in common is how the lovers met their tragic ends and were immortalized forever. The Aztecs believed there were once two lovers known as Popocatépetl and Iztaccíhuatl.

In the village of Tlaxcaltecas (which you may recall was the enemy of the Aztecs), there lived a chief with his beautiful daughter Iztaccíhuatl. As the daughter of the chief, she was a princess and she was beautiful in a way that the others were not; her beauty was unable to be compared to anything else and there were many suitors that wished to have her throughout the lands.

Yet, despite all the attention she received because of her beauty, she only had eyes for one of her father's warriors – the striking Popocatépetl who she admired dearly. Her love was not unrequited and after they had each confessed their love, Popocatépetl asked the chief of Tlaxcaltecas if he could marry her. The chief agreed that the two could be wed, with the only condition that Popocatépetl must come back to Tlaxcaltecas victorious from his battle.

The warrior accepted the terms and went to fight, happy to fight for his city and then return to his one true love afterwards. Some time passed over the course of the battle and the princess did not hear anything about what had happened to her true love. Eventually, the princess heard news that he had fallen in battle and was devastated.

With the news that her future husband had died – and the only person that she could imagine spending the rest of her life with – the princess in turn died from heartbreak; overwhelmed from the fact she would never again see him.

However, Popocatépetl had not in fact fallen in battle as this was a lie that one of his enemies had told the princess; hoping that he would get Iztaccíhuatl all to himself. He disappeared and then of course Popocatépetl returned.

Popocatépetl had returned victorious; having slain all the cities enemies in battle and eagerly went home to begin setting about marrying his one true love. Yet, when he returned he was heartbroken to discover that his love had died – perished from heartbreak.

Bound by grief, he decided that he would honour their proclamation of love for each other still; even though they were not wed – they had confessed their feelings and Popocatépetl felt them to be true and sincere enough that their love would last forever. As such, Popocatépetl commanded a tomb to be build in her honour. He wanted her to be immortalized forever.

Workers set about building the monumental tomb that Popocatépetl had commanded. Aztecs believed that it was huge and said to have been so big, it eventually created a mountain.

Once the tomb was built, Popocatépetl carried the body of Iztaccíhuatl to it, and knelt in front of her, watching her sleep. He was unable to leave her side, bound by his love and felt like he should watch over her for the rest of eternity.

As such, he remained there and the legend says that he is still there to this day, watching over her.

Due tot eh amount of time passed, stone and snow eventually bound both their bodies; creating two volcanos known as Popocatépetl and Iztaccíhuatl. Popocatépetl is still active to this day and that is why the Aztecs believed that the volcano still erupts – even now – as he is still there, watching over his love and remembering the passion that they both once held together.

The Rag-Picker and The Priest

In the Aztec legends there was once a Nahua rag-picker as explained by Native Languages (Online, n.d.). One day, this man found a book near Huitzilopochtli's temple of worship when he was working. It was a beautifully decorated book, and it had glyphs inside that the rag-picker could not understand.

As he couldn't understand it, he took it to a priest at the temple and asked him to explain the glyphs to him. The priest was surprised, but excitedly explained that the book foretold of magical treasures that were hidden inside the pyramid. As such, both the men agreed that they would seek out the treasure and split it evenly between them.

The treasure apparently laid hidden under the 93rd step on the pyramid, so both of them counted the steps, until they got to the 93rd one. Sure enough, after they both removed the 93rd step, they found a casket inside.

The casket contained sacred treasures, and the priest was amazed, but he knew that because of the sacredness of the treasures, they would be no good in the hands of the rag-picker. Inside the casket, there was a sorcerer's book, a wand, a mirror that could see the future, an almanac, a rattle and a drumstick. The rag-picker watched as the priest handled the things until the priest turned to him.

He told him that the items were sacred, and of no value to a rag-picker, but agreed to pay the rag-picker for the items instead. The rag-picker agreed, but as the priest counted out the gold he was going to give to the rag-picker, the rag-picker used the wand to kill him.

He was irritated the priest had implied he couldn't use the items; and as such had killed him by attacking him with the wand. He stole the money that the priest was going to give him, then disposed of the body before looking at the various objects that he had acquired.

Of course, the objects were very valuable; but as the priest had said the rag-picker couldn't understand how to use them. He tried to learn, but instead he felt as if they were cursed. He used the mirror to look into the future, but couldn't comprehend what it was showing him. He shook the rattle, and strange, odd sounds would escape it; which frightened him terribly.

Eventually the rag-picker could not sleep as well, as spirits would disturb his sleep and keep him awake. He decided that he would dispose of the items for good; hoping that he would finally get some solace.

He gathered the items, returned them to the casket and threw them all in the lake. Yet, to his horror the priests emerged and caught it.

The priest took out the want and hit the rag-picker, where he instantly died as a result. The priest treasured the items for the remainder of his days, and kept the sacred items with him wherever he went.

The cempasúchil Flower

The doomed story of Popocatépetl and Iztaccíhuatl isn't the only popular love story that the Aztecs shared. There was also the story of Xóchitl and Huitzilin.

Both of the Aztecs grew up together, and they were pretty much joint at the hip. Both of the young Aztecs loved to explore, but there was one place that they always seemed to venture.

There was a mountain that both of the children would climb and offer flowers to the sun god at the time (Tonatiuh). Tonatiuh graciously accepted their sweet offerings and as a result sun rays would shine over the two.

As they grew older, their love blossomed and then on one fateful day, atop the same mountain they offered flowers to for the sun god Tonatiuh, they proclaimed their love forever.

Shortly after, a great war broke out and Xóchitl and Huitzilin were separated. After some time of not hearing anything about her lover, Xóchitl eventually learned that Huitzilin had died in battle.

Heartbroken by the loss of the one she thought her love would blossom with forever, she climbed atop the mountain where they used to offer flowers together to the sun god Tonatiuh. In the depths of despair, Xóchitl asked if the Tonatiuh could reunite her with her one true love.

To her surprise, Tonatiuh heard her prays and shone down upon her; turning her into a beautiful flower that was just as bright as the sun shone. Then, a hummingbird came and touched the flower with it's beak.

Huitzilin had been reincarnated as a hummingbird; and together their love would remain eternal, as long as the flowers and hummingbirds continued to exist. This flower can still be found today and is known now as the Day of the Dead flower; cempasúchil.

Chapter Nine
Games

The Aztecs had many games that they would use to pass the time. The games varied dependent on their social standing, but most of all, as the Aztecs heavily admired and worshipped the gods, all games represented some of their beliefs.

Ullamaliztli

In the game of Ullamaliztli, the players would compete in a court that was in an I shape. The court was called a Tlachtli, and a person would have to shoot a ball through a hoop that was on opposite walls in the court. Whichever team scored first, would win the game.

However; this is not quite as simple as it sounds, as the players would need to play the game on their knees; they would also have to pass the ball to one another using their shoulders, heads, hips and even their knees. As such it was quite a difficult game!

The ball used was also a large rubber ball, and based on the players it was sometimes hard to score. The ballcourt was located in the centre of Tenochtitlan and when it was played it held cultural and religious significance for the Aztecs.

They perceived the game as a battle of the day and night that the gods themselves were constantly fighting; the court represented the underworld where the sun was forced to pass each night and the fight of the gods to keep the world turning and to ensure the sun still passed to make it through another day. As the court of Tlachtli was near the temple, it was also thought that the ball itself represented a human sacrifice – with the ball being the head.

Historians often argue about who was sacrificed at the end of the game – but one of the teams usually met their end when a game was won, being sacrificed by the temple accordingly.

Although the game of Ullamaliztli was often played near the temple, others enjoyed it for recreational purposes as well. Children, commoners and people of various classes often played the game when it wasn't played competitively.

Patolli

Another popular game in the times of the Aztec empire was known as Patolli. This game was like that of a board game, and also had some cultural and religious significance, much like Ullamaliztli.

The number 52 was prominent in the game; and this is notable as the Aztecs believed that the world might've ended after another 52 years. In addition to this throughout the game you had to make sacrifices to the dice – much like the Aztecs would make human sacrifices to the gods.

The game was in the shape of a cross, and there were holes in it. In total, the board was split into 52 squares and players had five/six beans they would use as dice with white holes put into it (or a normal dice), and they would also have pebbles that were red or blue.

Each player would take turn rolling the dice/throwing the beans and move the pebbles along the board gradually. The aim of the game was to get to the end of the board before the other player.

Totoloque

Another popular game was known as Totloque. In this game, a slab of gold was presented and the players would have to try and hit the target with little gold pallets. Each player would receive five tries to attempt to hit the gold slab and the player with the most hits would win the game.

Oftentimes, this would be a betting game; notably the late Montezuma II was said to have played this with Hernan Cortes before he tried to concur the Aztecs or kidnap him. The emperor was said to have lost the games, but was said to have not cared much for the loss.

Chapter Ten
What Happened to the Aztecs?

Even though the Spanish conquered the Aztec empire itself, there are still some questions on how the Aztecs seemed to disappear completely from history. Hernan Cortes came with an army and managed to overthrow them completely.

What History Says

Historians and experts say that Henan Cortes trained troops near Tenochtitlan, but he also made sure to make allies with the Aztec's enemies. Before Cortes slayed the emperor Montezuma, he made friends with the nearby Tlascalans who, at the time, were engaged in a war with the Aztecs.

Cortes and his army then went to the capital, but Montezuma at the time didn't order an attack on the Spanish. The emperor believed that it was Quetzalcoatl – one of the gods that once walked in human form and the Aztecs believed would return one day (one of the myths said that he disappeared after sleeping with his sister and would return some day).

Due to the above, the Aztecs welcomed Hernan Cortes and his army with open arms, treating them as honoured guests. Cortes used this to his advantage, quickly capturing the emperor. Following this, he demanded that the Aztecs step down and allow him to take control of Tenochtitlan, but they fought him off and as a result of this Montezuma ended up dying in the crossfire.

Cuauhtémoc ended up becoming the new emperor of Tenochtitlan as the other Aztecs managed to force Hernan Cortes and his army out of the city. Yet, given the amount of allies Cortes had gained, he travelled back to Tenochtitlan and took over empire once and for all.

Following the above, it is believed that Hernan Cortes and his army burned down the empire – destroying everything he could in his path that would've belonged to the Aztecs. Of course, some of the Aztec people still remained but sadly, they began to die out through other means.

Disease

After the Aztecs had been conquered the city began to be rebuilt as part of the Spanish empire in Mexico. However, they began to fall ill because of several diseases that the Spanish had brought with them at the time.

Although the Aztecs had been ahead of their time in many ways – they were not able to fight off these diseases. Smallpox, mumps and measles all raced through what was once known as the city of Tenochtitlan and as such the Aztecs fell victim to it's grip of death.

Unable to deal with diseases of this scale, many of the Aztecs died as a result of this. It is believed that in addition to the western diseases above, the Aztecs also fell to another mysterious epidemic.

There was a national pandemic and was likened to be similar to that of the bubonic plague. Apparently, it killed off almost all of the remaining Aztec population. Nobody knew exactly where the plague had originated from, but the fact was that it killed off almost all the remaining Aztec citizens.

Droughts

The Aztecs had the incredible ability to grow food and they felt they were blessed to have received as much rainfall as they did throughout the years. However, shortly after they were conquered and when the diseases began to come about the new city went through a drought.

Not many of the Aztecs remained, but the last of their people were thought to die out as a result of the above. They had already had to endure the battle that had waged in the city that they lost and then there was the disease that ravaged it. Now with the droughts, they didn't stand much of a chance for survival.

As a result of the droughts that swept through the land, it is thought that the remainder of the Aztecs ended up dying out due to not being able to feed most of their population. Due to the drought, water supplies also dried up; so the remainder of the Aztecs were left both starving and thirsty.

Are Any Still Alive?

Although the original Aztec empire fell and the majority of the population was killed, there are still descendants of the Aztecs that live in Mexico to this day.

Today, the Aztecs are known as the Nahua instead, and they live in several small communities throughout Mexico. Although their religious practises and festivals are very different to what it once was, they still celebrate their cultural heritage (although, without the human sacrifices!).

Chapter Eleven
What is Left of the Aztecs today?

Traditions

Although the Aztecs were concurred by the Spanish in the 16th century and most died out because of the other things they were forced to endure (such as the droughts, famine, disease, etc) some elements of the Aztec culture can still be found today in Mexico. When the Spanish conquered the Aztec empire, they brought with them Christianity and this led to a merge of the beliefs in a great deal of cases. As such, as much as the Spanish were determined to wipe out – what they believed – the barbaric and pagan beliefs of the Aztecs, some people still turn to certain deities to this day for aid and follow some of the ancient practises.

Nowadays (as mentioned previously), most of the descendants of what was known as the Aztecs are now referred to as Nahua who live in Mexico. Although they traditionally worship Christian beliefs, if they are sick they may seek out a healer who will give them incense to get better. Sometimes, to this day blood sacrifices are still practised as well (however, nowadays animals are sacrificed rather than people!). In addition to this, it is also known that they may offer patients herbs or even do prayers and incantations – much like the ancient Aztecs would have done back during their time.

Also interestingly enough, the Nahua people are also very adept at agriculture and grow many different things. In particular, they grow some of what their Aztec ancestors once grew to create their kingdom such as corn/maize, tomatoes and peppers. Although, nowadays they usually also grow more popular items such as coffee, sugarcane and rice – as is more popular.

In addition to the above, the classes back in the times of Aztec once separated cotton for the rich. As discussed previously although the Aztecs grew cotton – only those of a social standing were permitted to wear it. Now, weaving cotton and wool is still used to this day – both men and women can expertly weave and loom various different clothing or accessories.

Rituals

The most renown ritual that has been carried from the time of the Aztecs is the Day of the Dead; however, it has transformed into something more than it was in the times when the Aztecs existed.

Back in the times of the Aztec, they would use skulls to honor the dead, but now something like that is still used in what is now known as the Day of the Dead festival – or Día De Muertos. However, when the Spanish took over Tenochtitlan they brought their Christian beliefs with them and attempted to change the practises of what the Aztecs had celebrated to what was known as "All Saints Day" and "All Souls Day" that fell in the beginning of November.

Yet, given the practises that the Aztecs used, the beliefs of the two different faiths were merged together to create Día De Muertos. Parts of the Aztec culture can still be seen in this ritual in a great deal of ways; for example all the elements are present in the altars that the families of the deceased make;

- Water/alcohol will be placed on the altar
- Food will be put on the grave as well as an offering
- A fire will be lit – usually a candle
- Wind is shown through artwork that is produced

These four elements were quite renown through Aztec culture, as such the fact they're used in a festival to celebrate the dead to this day should be fairly unsurprising.

Lastly, the biggest take away from the festival is the marigold flower which is used to decorate all the altars in Mexico. The flowers have another name – the cempasúchil flower which was a legend from Aztec times as discussed previously. In terms of the Day of the Dead festival, Mexicans now believe that these flowers guide the souls back home for those that they've lost.

Although the Day of the Dead is the most well-known festival, there are many others that the Mexicans celebrate still that remain from the Aztec times. One of which is they celebrate the last emperor from the time the Aztecs reigned – known as the Cuauhtémoc festival.

This festival is traditionally celebrated in summer and is celebrated in front of the statue of the last emperor of the Aztecs. Following this, many tell the story of his life in Spanish and the other languages that are in Mexico today.

After the above, dances follow – with the dancers being adorned in elaborate feathered headdresses and beads. Notably, they carry pictures of both saints and Jesus Christ; representing how the Aztec culture and Spanish one blended together to create what it is today.

The people of Mexico also pay homage to what was once the annual 52 year celebration. This has been changed however, to now be called the "New Fire" ceremony which many partake in.

Instead of being celebrated every 52 years, this ceremony is now celebrated once every year instead. It is hosted in a different city every year and they pass the "fire" from the old city to the new city. The fire is considered as sacred and the people that last hosted the fire travel by foot to bring it to the new city.

Much like the other festivals, there is dancing, music and rituals that they go through to pass the fire from one place to another. In some ways; the Aztec culture can still be seen in this ceremony – with the fire being protected all year round by one community and being given to another is much like the way the gods tried to nourish the sun each year.

The next festival that the Mexicans celebrate in honour of the Aztecs is the festival of Xilonen. Groups of people dance together during this festival and people wear clothing adorned with Aztec symbols.

People come together to celebrate their heritage and it is also believed to be a rite of passage for girls becoming women. The young girls who partake in the festival have a guide that teaches and supports them, helping them navigate the world of blossoming into a young woman and also helps to teach them the Aztec dances that were once used.

Although the modern day interpretation is quite admirable; how the Aztecs once celebrated it were quite gruesome in comparison. Xilonen was one of the Goddesses that the ancient Aztecs worshipped (also known as Chicomecoatl).

Back in the times of the Aztecs, during her festival, unmarried girls would wear their hair loose and carry green corn to offer the goddess. A slave girl would be chosen, and dressed up as the goddess and then she would be sacrificed to nourish Xilonen accordingly.

These days the festival is quite different, and no sacrifices are required! Yet, the dances that the women do are still practised and the celebration is renown for it's focus on women's navigation through womanhood.

Games

Some games have survived ancient Aztec times as well – one in particular is the popular ball game that the Aztecs used to play – known as Ullamaliztli.

Nowadays however, players do not have to worry about being sacrificed at the end of the day and it has been shortened to Ulama.

It is a little different to what it used to be and the players wear more protection nowadays (after all, being hit by a rubber ball certainly isn't pleasant!). They usually play in a court and try to score goals with the rubber ball and it consists of two teams.

It's amazing that a game such as this has managed to survive such a long time and can still be seen played today – even if some of the rules have changed slightly.

Clothing and Costumes

The people of Mexico wear clothing that is just like any other country; some styles they use from Europe or native countries. However, interestingly enough some remains of the Aztec dress still exist in their every day society.

One of the most popular is the Tilmatli which is a modern style of the Aztec clothing. Whilst the ancient Aztecs wore only the Tilmatli, people of today often wear it over their other clothes instead. In addition to this, it is often has many different functions and people can wear it as a blouse, a shawl – and if you really want to – people can use it as a cape.

Something which is almost similar to the above is the poncho which can be seen today. They often are also worn over the other clothes and they often have intricate designs that you would not find elsewhere.

During some ceremonies costumes are often worn as well dependent on which one. For example in the celebration of the last Aztec ruler, lavish hairdressers are usually worn alongside gold and silver clothing.

Other than the above, not many costumes can be found today from the Aztec culture outside of the Mexican ceremonies celebrating the long gone civilisation.

Art

As mentioned previously the Aztecs didn't particularly care much for art; as everything held a purpose and as such statues, art and what not was seen more for religious purposes.

However, some have been preserved to this day and there are still statues or other forms of art that remain from the empire. Sculptures of the Gods still remain to this day and can be found in many places in Mexico still.

In addition to the above there are other forms of art that have survived the last five hundred years such as mosaics, pottery and even poetry! All of which can be found in museums to this day.

Of course, the modern day Nahau, of what remains of the Aztecs can be seen to incorporate the Aztec arts into their day-to-day lives. Leaving some remains of the long-lost civilisation such as patterns, or depictions of the gods that were once thought to rule the world.

Museums

There are many museums all over the world that include pieces of the Aztec empire where you can learn more about them. In Mexico alone there are two main ones that you can go visit that contain a wealth of resources, not including the historical landmarks that remain of the civilisation.

The first museum that should be visited if you wish to learn more about the history of the Aztecs is the Museo Nacional de Antropología which can be found in Bosque de Chapultepec. Some of the exhibits that it has includes:

- The Aztec Calendar Stone
- The Headdress of Moctezuma
- A model of the city of Tenochtitlan
- A statue of Chalchiuhtilcue

Although these are just a few, they are all hold a great deal of cultural significance and are all tokens of the long-gone era of the Aztec Empire.

Following the above, another must-visit temple is the Templo Mayor Museum. This was once where the temple at the centre of Tenochtitlan laid – the very same spot that the Aztecs believed Huitzilopochtli had guided them to in order to create the city.

The museum and the excavated temple has many remains of the once great empire. The most notable is the stone carving of Coyolxauhqui or the monoliths of Tlaltecuhtli.

Lastly, the must-see part of the Templo Mayor museum is most likely the "Wall of Skulls" Which contains a sculpture of stone skulls that show the many people the Aztecs sacrificed in their rituals.

Other notable museums or places that contain parts of the Aztec culture are the Museo de la Ciudad de Mexico and the Anahuacalli Museum. Both of these are in Mexico and able to be visited.

Of course, there are other museums all over the world that still hold exhibits dedicated to the Aztecs. A good example of this is the British Museum located in the united kingdom, that holds an array of Aztec treasures and history people can explore and learn from.

Do you know that I have also an audiobook series exclusively on **<u>Audible</u>**?

Scan here to find out more!

References

Adams, S. (2011). *Reasons for the Fall of the Aztec Empire*. Seminar Paper: GRIN Verlag

Aguilar-Moreno, M. (2007). *Handbook to life in the Aztec world*. Oxford ; New York: Oxford University Press.

Aztec Empire. (n.d.). *Cultural Maps*. [online] Available   at: https://aztecempirepcep.weebly.com/cultural-maps.html.

Aztec-history.com. (2019). *Aztec Creation Story*. [online] Available at: http://www.aztec-history.com/aztec-creation-story.html.

Blog Contributor (2017). *The Aztecs on Happiness, Pleasure and the Good Life*. [online] Blog of the APA. Available at: https://blog.apaonline.org/2017/02/22/aztecs-on-happiness/

Carrasco, D. and Sessions, S. (2011). *Daily Life of the Aztecs*. Santa Barbara, Calif.: Greenwood.

Collections, S. (n.d.). *Tarlton Law Library: Exhibit - Aztec and Maya Law: Aztec Political Structure*. [online] tarlton.law.utexas.edu. Available at: https://tarlton.law.utexas.edu/aztec-and-maya-law/aztec-political-structure#:~:text=The%20Aztec%20empire%20was%20made.

Cutright, R.E. (2021). *The story of food in the human past : how what we ate made us who we are*. Tuscaloosa: The University Of Alabama Press.

Ducksters.com. (2019). *Aztec Empire for Kids: Society*. [online] Available at: https://www.ducksters.com/history/aztec_empire/society.php.

Jarus, O. (2017). *Tenochtitlán: History of Aztec Capital*. [online] livescience.com. Available at: https://www.livescience.com/34660-tenochtitlan.html.

Laack, I. (2019). *Aztec religion and art of writing : investigating embodied meaning, indigenous semiotics, and the Nahua sense of reality.* Leiden ; Boston: Brill.

Morganelli, A. (2006). *The biography of chocolate.* New York, Ny: Crabtree Pub. Co.

Mythopedia. (n.d.). *Quetzalcoatl.* [online] Available at: https://mythopedia.com/aztec-mythology/gods/quetzalcoatl/.

Read, K.A. and Gonzalez, J.J. (2000). *Mesoamerican Mythology: A Guide to the Gods, Heroes, Rituals, and Beliefs of Mexico and Central America.* Oxford University Press: New York.

Vickery, K. (2018). *Minor Gods and Aztec Demons.* [online] Manzanillo Sun. Available at: https://www.manzanillosun.com/minor-gods-and-aztec-demons/ [Accessed 18 Apr. 2021].

Wikipedia. (2021). *Aztec religion.* [online] Available at: https://en.wikipedia.org/wiki/Aztec_religion#:~:text=The%20cosmology%20of%20Aztec%20religion [Accessed 15 Apr. 2021].

World History Encyclopedia. (n.d.). *Aztec Food & Agriculture.* [online] Available at:

https://www.worldhistory.org/article/723/aztec-food--agriculture/ [Accessed 15 Apr. 2021].

www.mesoweb.com. (n.d.). *Myths and Legends of the Aztecs.* [online] Available at: http://www.mesoweb.com/features/aztecs/migration_text.html [Accessed 16 Apr. 2021].

www.mexicolore.co.uk. (n.d.). *A Rabbit in the Moon?* [online] Available at: https://www.mexicolore.co.uk/aztecs/aztefacts/rabbit-in-the-moon [Accessed 17 Apr. 2021].

www.mexicolore.co.uk. (n.d.). *Basic Aztec facts: AZTEC HOUSES.* [online] Available at: https://www.mexicolore.co.uk/aztecs/kids/aztec-houses.

www.mt-oceanography.info. (n.d.). *Science, civilization and society.* [online] Available at: https://www.mt-oceanography.info/science+society/lectures/illustrations/lecture18/montezumaII.html [Accessed 17 Apr. 2021].

www.native-languages.org. (n.d.). *An Aztec Legend.* [online] Available at: http://www.native-languages.org/aztecstory.htm [Accessed 17 Apr. 2021].

Additional Reading

Although I have a wealth of knowledge of the Aztecs, during my time in writing this book I felt it essential to undertake the task of reading and broadening my knowledge thoroughly. As a result of this, I would also recommend to anyone who wishes to learn more about the Aztecs to also read the below books, which I have during my time and journey in learning about Aztec culture.

- Mexican and Central American Mythology by Irene Nicholson

- Society and Laws of the Aztec Empire by Standford Mc   Krause

- The Fate of Earthly Things: Aztec Gods and God-Bodies by Molly H. Bassett

- Aztec Thought and Culture by Miguel Leon-Portilla

- Life in the Aztec Empire by Stanford Mc Krause

Appendix

A -- Timeline

1100	Aztecs leave northern Mexico
1200	Aztecs arrive in Mexico Valley
1250	Aztecs settle in Chapultepec, but are run out of the city
1325	Aztecs find Tenochtitlan and it is founded
1350	Aztecs build canals/causeways
1375	Acamapichtli becomes first leader/king/emperor of the Aztecs
1427	Itzcoatl becomes the 4th ruler, and helps Tenochtitlan continue to blossom
1428	Aztecs form an alliance with Texcocans and the Tacubans. Together, they defeat the Tepanecs.
1440 - 1469	Becoming the fifth leader, Montezuma I begins to help the empire continue to thrive.
1452	A flood envelopes the city and the Aztecs suffer famine and starvation as a result.
1487	The Aztecs complete the Great Temple of Tenochtitlan dedicated to their Gods. They begin offering human sacrifices.
1502	Montezuma II became the next ruler of the Empire; becoming the ninth.
1517	A comet raced through the sky, Aztec priests assumed that the Aztecs were doomed because of this.
1519	Hernan Cortes arrived in Tenochtitlan and kidnapped Montezuma II. The leader was later killed.
1520	Cuauhtémoc became the last leader and the Aztecs were attacked by Cortes and the Tlaxcala
1521 – 1522	Cortes defeated the Aztecs, and the Spanish rebuilt the city with the Aztecs disappearing forever.

Did you enjoy the book? If so, please **leave a positive review** directly on Amazon!

And if you still want to learn more, check out the other books in the *Easy History* series: An exciting journey back in time and a unique chance to meet your ancestors!

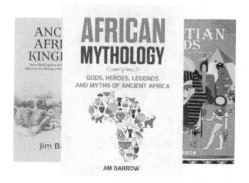

Scan this QR Code to find out more:

Do you want to get rid of stress and learn something new in the process? Discover the new series **"Myths and History Coloring Books"** and you'll find the perfect way to do that. So what are you waiting for?

Scan the following QR code and take a look!

Made in the USA
Las Vegas, NV
06 October 2023

78684894R00066